Little Pebble™

Habitats

All About
Wetlands

by Christina Mia Gardeski

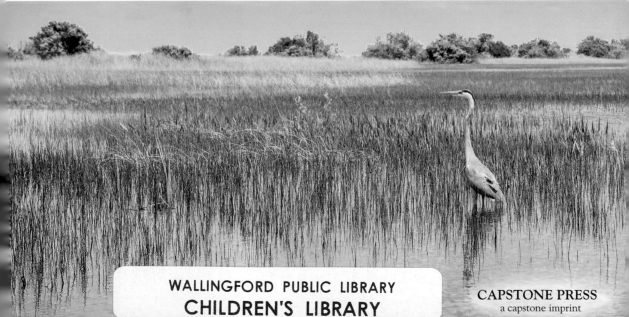

CAPSTONE PRESS
a capstone imprint

Little Pebble is published by Capstone Press,
1710 Roe Crest Drive, North Mankato, Minnesota 56003
www.mycapstone.com

Library of Congress Cataloging-in-Publication Data
Names: Gardeski, Christina Mia, author.
Title: All about wetlands / by Christina Mia Gardeski.
Description: North Mankato, Minnesota : Capstone Press, [2018] |
    Series: Little pebble. Habitats | Audience: Ages 4–8.
Identifiers: LCCN 2017031564 (print) | LCCN 2017045289 (ebook) |
    ISBN 9781515797715 (eBook PDF) | ISBN 9781515797593 (hardcover) |
    ISBN 9781515797678 (paperback)
Subjects: LCSH: Wetland ecology—Juvenile literature. | Wetlands—Juvenile literature.
Classification: LCC QH541.5.M3 (ebook) | LCC QH541.5.M3 G38 2018 (print) |
    DDC 577.68—dc23
LC record available at https://lccn.loc.gov/2017031564

Editorial Credits
Marissa Kirkman, editor; Juliette Peters (cover) and Charmaine Whitman (interior), designers;
Eric Gohl, media researcher; Katy LaVigne, production specialist

Photo Credits
Getty Images: Doxieone Photography, 17; iStockphoto: maimai, 20; Shutterstock: AlxYago, 9, baxys, 21, Dj7, 11, HelloRF Zcool, 5, lafoto, 7, lazyllama, 15, Melok, back cover, interior (reeds illustration), Michael G McKinne, 19, N_Belonogov, cover, Romrodphoto, 1, sahua d, 16, skynetphoto, 13

Printed and bound in the USA.
010916S18

Table of Contents

What Is a Wetland?

A wetland is a low land.

It is filled with water.

Rain falls.

Tides roll in.

A wetland holds the water.
This stops floods.

Marsh

Grass grows in a marsh.

The water can be shallow.

A marsh is a wet habitat.

Crabs lay eggs here.

Fish hide.

crab

Swamp

Trees grow in a swamp.

The water can be deep.

Tree trunks are thick.

Ducks nest here.

Alligators swim.

Bog

Moss grows in a bog.

The land is soft and wet.

moss

Plants rot in a bog.

Insects eat the plants.

Frogs eat the insects.

frog

Glossary

bog—a wetland with wet and soft ground where moss grows

flood—water that overflows onto dry land

habitat—the home of a plant or animal

marsh—a shallow wetland where grass grows

moss—small, low plants without flowers that grow in bogs

shallow—not deep

swamp—a deep wetland where trees grow

tide—the in and out flow of water in an ocean or river

trunk—the center stem of a tree from bottom to top, separate from its branches

Read More

Arnold, Quinn M. *Wetlands.* Seedlings. Mankato, Minn.: Creative Education, 2016.

Statts, Leo. *Alligators.* Swamp Animals. Minneapolis: Abdo Zoom, 2017.

Waxman, Laura Hamilton. *Life in a Wetland.* Biomes Alive! Minneapolis: Bellwether Media, 2016.

Internet Sites

Use FactHound to find Internet sites related to this book.

Visit www.facthound.com

Just type in 9781515797593 and go.

Super-cool stuff!

Check out projects, games and lots more at
www.capstonekids.com

Index